# Everybody's BOOK

## THE STORY OF THE SARAJEVO HAGGADAH

Linda Leopold Strauss

ILLUSTRATED BY Tim Smart

KAR-BEN
PUBLISHING

**For Bill, who gave me the space to write. —L.L.S.**

**For my mother, my partner, and my daughter, who inspire, delight, and teach me in equal measure. I love you all. —T.S.**

KAR-BEN PUBLISHING®
An imprint of Lerner Publishing Group, Inc.
241 First Avenue North
Minneapolis, MN 55401 USA

Website address: www.karben.com

Photographs on page 32 by Thomas Eisenstadt

Main body text set in Adobe Caslon Pro.
Typeface provided by Adobe Systems.

**Library of Congress Cataloging-in-Publication Data**

Names: Strauss, Linda Leopold, author. | Smart, Tim, illustrator.
Title: Everybody's book : the story of the Sarajevo Haggadah / by Linda Leopold Strauss ; illustrated by Tim Smart.
Description: Minneapolis : Kar-Ben Publishing, 2024. | Audience: Ages 4–8 | Audience: Grades K–1 | Summary: "The true story of the famous Sarajevo Haggadah begins long ago in Spain. Used for centuries and declared a treasure, people of many faiths have protected the Haggadah up to this day"— Provided by publisher.
Identifiers: LCCN 2023004334 (print) | LCCN 2023004335 (ebook) | ISBN 9781728486468 (library binding) | ISBN 9798765613627 (epub)
Subjects: LCSH: Sarajevo Haggadah—Juvenile literature. | Haggadah—Juvenile literature. | Passover— Juvenile literature.
Classification: LCC BM674.79 .S77 2024 (print) | LCC BM674.79 (ebook) | DDC 296.4/5371—dc23/ eng/20230213

LC record available at https://lccn.loc.gov/2023004334
LC ebook record available at https://lccn.loc.gov/2023004335

Manufactured in China
1-52564-50756-4/7/2023

**SARAJEVO, BOSNIA. 1995.** Fighter jets flew overhead, bombing the city into rubble. But even with war raging around them, the people of Sarajevo were worrying about a book.

The book was special from the beginning.

Around 1350, a Jewish wedding took place in Spain. The bride and groom received a gift, a haggadah for their Passover celebrations.

The haggadah was hand-painted and hand-lettered, with decorations of copper and gold. It told the story of the Israelite slaves' escape from Egypt in ancient days. It also held beautiful paintings of other Bible stories, with elaborate images of birds and dogs and even dragons.

The family used the haggadah each year for the Passover seder, the ancient Jewish celebration of freedom.

"Let everyone who is hungry come and eat," say the ancient words of the haggadah.

For many years, Jews in Spain had lived in peace alongside their Catholic neighbors. But by the late 1400s, during the Spanish Inquisition, things had changed.

It was a frightening time. Spanish Jews were forced to become Christians. Those who refused had to leave Spain. Jewish books and religious treasures were destroyed. The family that owned the special haggadah escaped, taking the book with them.

As years went by, the haggadah was passed from generation to generation. It found its way to Italy, then north to Bosnia. Families spilled wine on it during Passover seders. A child practiced writing numbers and Hebrew letters on its beautiful pages.

By 1894, the family that owned the haggadah had fallen on hard times, so they decided to sell the haggadah.

The National Museum in Sarajevo, Bosnia, bought the haggadah. Scholars declared it a treasure, an important piece of history, one of the oldest and most beautiful books of its kind in the world. It became known as the Sarajevo Haggadah. Bosnians were very proud of it.

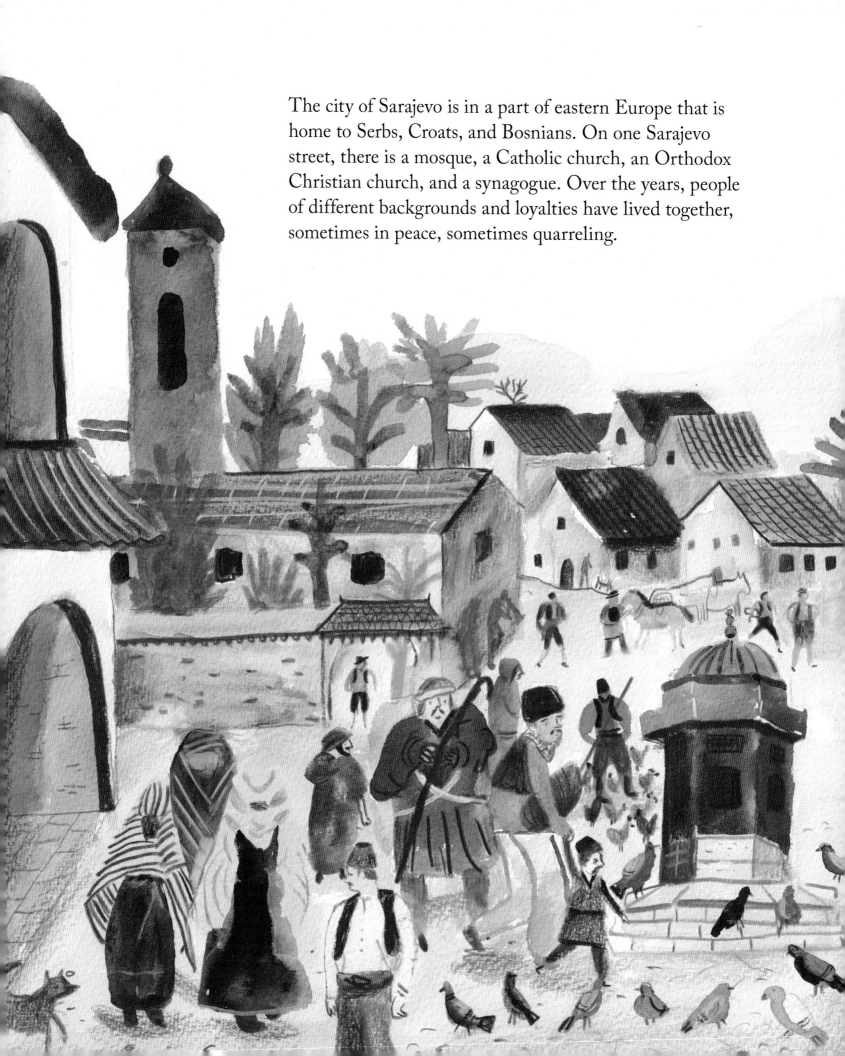

The city of Sarajevo is in a part of eastern Europe that is home to Serbs, Croats, and Bosnians. On one Sarajevo street, there is a mosque, a Catholic church, an Orthodox Christian church, and a synagogue. Over the years, people of different backgrounds and loyalties have lived together, sometimes in peace, sometimes quarreling.

In 1941, as World War II swept across Europe, the Nazis invaded Sarajevo. The workers at the National Museum learned that a Nazi general was coming to steal the haggadah.

The workers decided not to give up the precious book. The museum's curator, a Muslim scholar, tucked the haggadah out of sight in the waistband of his trousers.

The Nazi general arrived at the museum and ordered the director to hand over the haggadah.

The director, a Croat Catholic, thought fast. He told the general that a Nazi colonel had already taken the haggadah. When the general demanded the colonel's name, the director said he hadn't been allowed to ask.

Not believing the director, the general had his soldiers search the museum, but they left empty-handed.

According to the story later told by the curator's wife, her husband came home for lunch with the haggadah. After lunch, she said, he drove it to a remote village, where an imam of a small mosque hid it among sacred Islamic texts.

No longer was this precious book just a Jewish treasure—it was everybody's treasure. And, throughout its history, it was protected by Muslims, Catholics, Orthodox Christians, and Jews.

After World War II ended, the curator brought
the Sarajevo Haggadah back to the museum.

But life in Sarajevo kept changing.

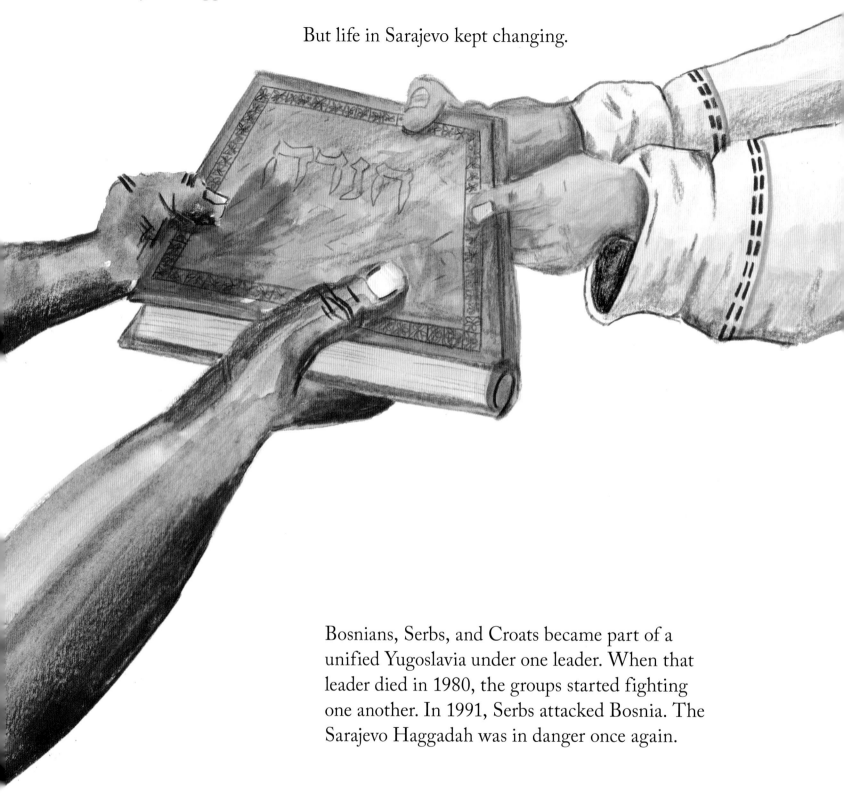

Bosnians, Serbs, and Croats became part of a
unified Yugoslavia under one leader. When that
leader died in 1980, the groups started fighting
one another. In 1991, Serbs attacked Bosnia. The
Sarajevo Haggadah was in danger once again.

The following year, the Serbs bombed the museum. It is said that a Muslim university professor ran to rescue the haggadah as shells crashed around him.

One story says he used a pickax to break open the safe where the book was kept.

According to another story, he called government soldiers to help him.

Still another story says he found the haggadah on the floor in the museum's basement, saving it from a flood caused by broken pipes.

Many books were destroyed in the fighting. The National and University Library in Sarajevo went up in flames.

As the building burned, brave volunteers passed books through the window to people waiting outside. Sarajevans formed a human chain to pass the books from person to person and get them away from the fire.

But only a small amount of the library's 1.5 million books were saved.

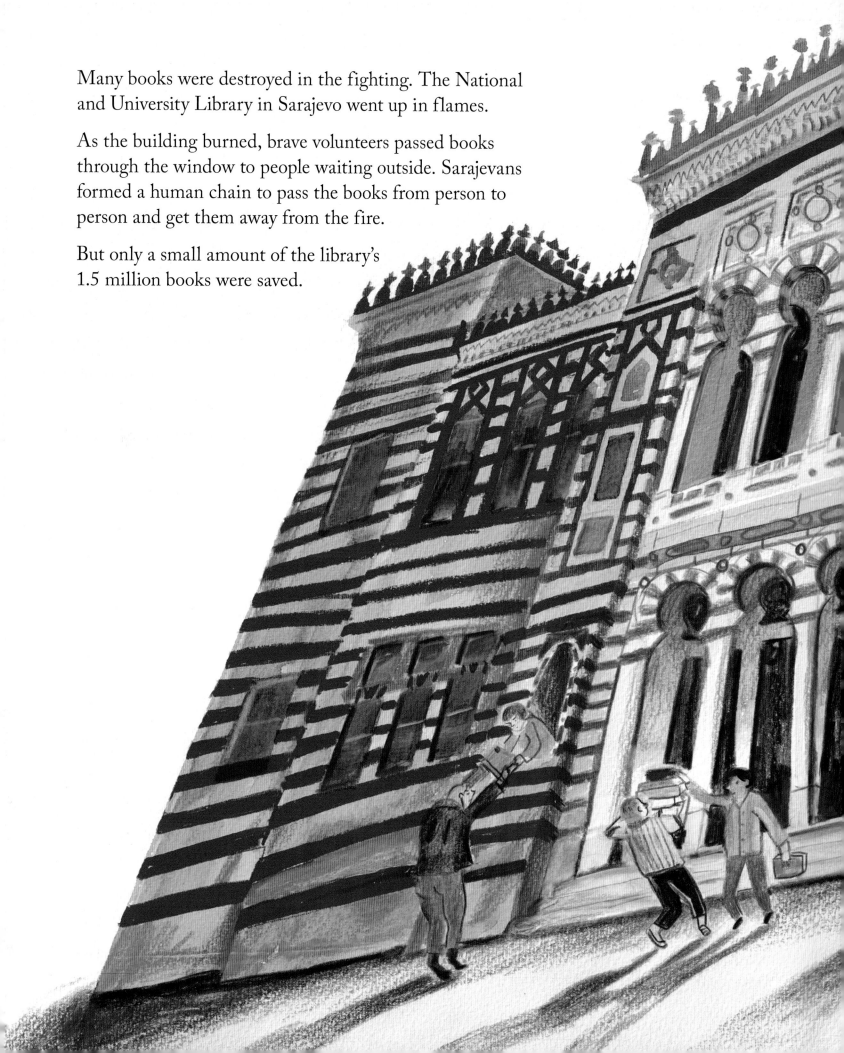

People all over the world were worried about one particular book, the Sarajevo Haggadah. Its story had spread far and wide. By now, it had become a symbol of hope—hope that kindness and understanding would be stronger than hatred. Remarkably, as the fighting continued, the haggadah remained safe in a secret location.

In the spring of 1995, during the Bosnian War, something wonderful took place. With bombs exploding and planes flying overhead, Christian Orthodox, Catholic, and Muslim religious leaders joined Jews at Sarajevo's only remaining synagogue for the Passover seder.

To everyone's surprise, the president of Bosnia, a Muslim, came to the synagogue with the Sarajevo Haggadah. Just for a moment. To show that the precious book was safe.

"Spend your holiday in peace," the president told the group gathered there.

Peace memorials were built when the war finally ended, and the haggadah was taken out of the underground vault in the National Bank where it had been hidden.

By this time, the book was nearly 650 years old. The United Nations donated money for the haggadah to be restored—brought back to its original condition as much as possible.

Its binding needed some repairs, but otherwise, the only damages to the haggadah were worn edges, wine stains, and the child's writing on its pages. The restorer left these things unchanged, as a way to honor the book's history.

The haggadah had been created for one family. But after centuries of use in Jewish homes, it had become a book that was cherished by the whole family of nations.

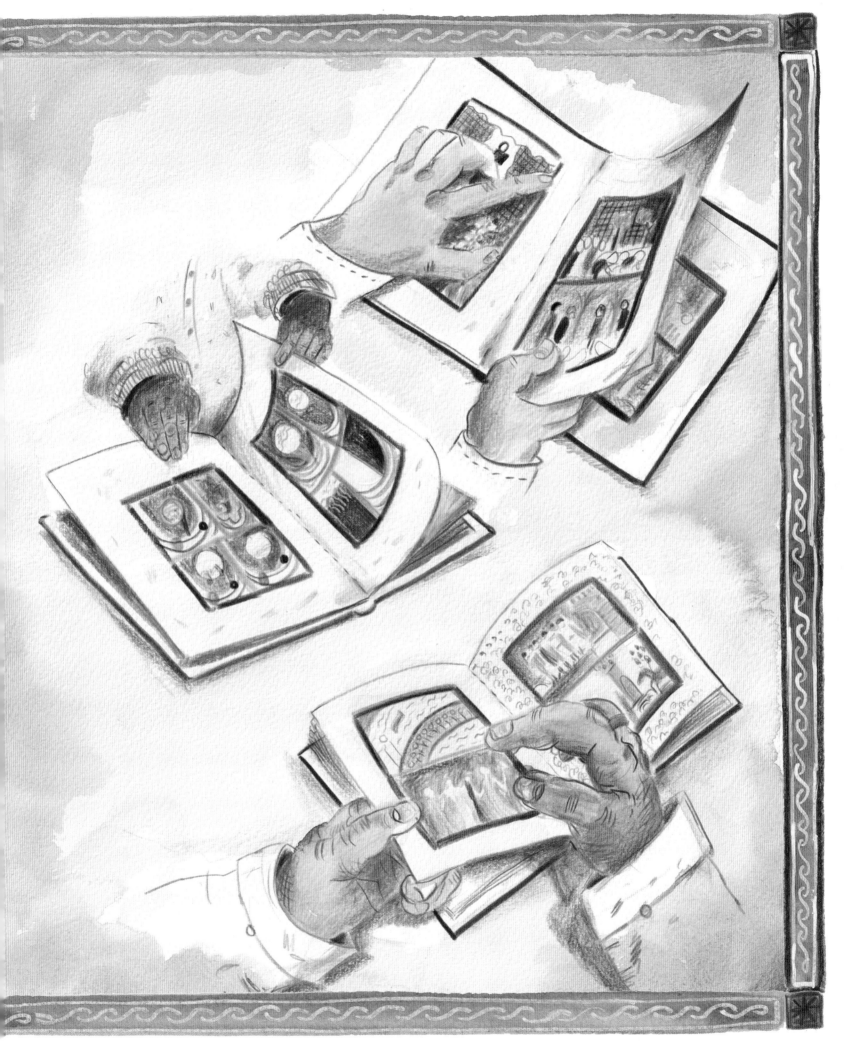

The Sarajevo Haggadah returned to the newly rebuilt Bosnian National Museum. It shares a room with ancient documents from Bosnia's other main religions—Christian Orthodoxy, Catholicism, and Islam. It had survived many dangers over hundreds of years because people of different backgrounds had cared for it and protected it.

**The Sarajevo Haggadah is everybody's book.**

## Author's Note

Haggadahs are the books used to tell the story of Passover at the Passover seder. The Hebrew word *haggadah* means "telling." The Sarajevo Haggadah is considered not only a haggadah but a great work of art. It is one of the oldest books of its kind in the world, and scholars have praised it as an important piece of history and have written about its remarkable illustrations.

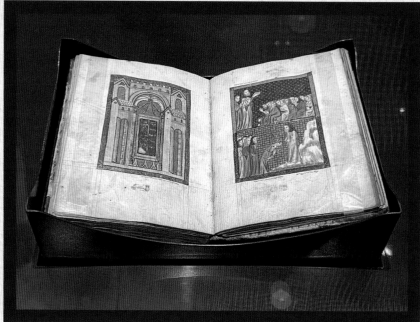

## About the Author

LINDA LEOPOLD STRAUSS is a graduate of Vassar College and Columbia University. She has been writing for young people for over forty years and has published twelve books and many stories for children. Her work has been translated into French, Italian, German, and Swedish. She lives with her husband in Cincinnati, Ohio.

## About the Illustrator

TIM SMART's illustrations draw inspiration from his experiences growing up by the ocean and climbing trees in forests. He likes making faces in the mirror, sitting by fires, rolling down hills, and chasing dogs. He hates surprising noises, sticky fingers, boring grown-ups, and birthdays. He lives in the United Kingdom.